SYNTHESIZERS
IN THE
ELEMENTARY
MUSIC CLASSROOM

AN INTEGRATED APPROACH

BY   JACKIE WIGGINS

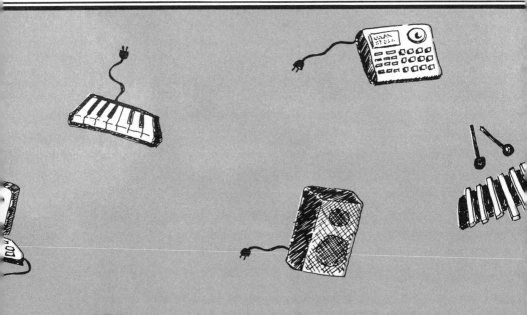

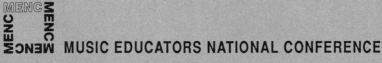

MENC MENC
MENC MENC MUSIC EDUCATORS NATIONAL CONFERENCE

Printed in the United States of America.

ISBN 1-56545-005-1

CONTENTS

INTRODUCTION

Synthesizers are very much a part of our lives. Many of our students own them—but often know very little about them. Many music teachers would like to bring synthesizers into their classrooms, but they are not sure of a synthesizer's place in an existing curriculum. This book is designed to provide teachers with some of the information they might need to do this successfully. Electronic instruments need only be one aspect of a classroom music curriculum to have their presence felt throughout the school music program. The flexibility of the equipment enables music teachers to integrate these instruments into any curriculum.

Today, music teachers are faced with an important decision. Should we make use of the technological advances in the world of music that exists outside of our music classrooms? As music educators, many of us feel unprepared to make this decision. The world of music is changing rapidly and there are so many new options that it is easy to feel overwhelmed and intimidated and choose to ignore the changes.

The prospect of using new equipment need not be frightening. It is important to recognize synthesizers and computers for what they are; they are simply new equipment. Technological advances need not alter the premises of music education. We are simply dealing with new tools for teaching. In the same way that music does not reside inside an instrument, learning does not reside inside computers and synthesizers. The important factor here is how we choose to use the new tools in teaching music.

Pedagogical decisions involving the use of new technology in the classroom are the same as pedagogical decisions regarding the use of traditional equipment. Teachers have experience with evaluating the appropriateness of new materials and ideas. A good teacher has program goals and purposes and a vision of the progress that each student should make as a result of participation in a music program. However, teachers must add to these goals and this vision a good understanding of the capabilities of the new equipment in order to make them fit into their programs.

Teachers who share a holistic view of general music education create programs designed to nurture the overall musicianship of the general public. They hope to encourage all students to develop the desire and the ability to hear more in all music and to be better equipped to make musical decisions in their own lives. Teachers who have created school programs designed to nurture this growth often shy away from the technological advances that are so often presented to music teachers.

Unfortunately, the way in which many of the new materials and devices have been marketed (as "cure-alls," as "general music packages," or even as complete curricula) has given the impression that using the new technology means relinquishing the right to make pedagogical decisions to the manufacturer. Much of what is available on the market focuses on the development of individual ability to read notation or to hear relationships between isolated pitches; neither of these goals is a priority for general music education. Many good music teachers have therefore chosen to ignore what the potential usefulness of modern equipment can do because they are unwilling to allow "packaged curricula" to replace their own.

In evaluating these new materials and equipment, teachers must ask themselves the same questions that they apply to conventional materials:

- What can I teach through this particular tool? How can I use it in the curriculum?
- Will it help my students to understand something important? Will it help them to continue to grow musically?
- Will it help to make my teaching more effective?
- Will it do a better job than conventional materials might? Will it do a comparable job in a more appealing way?
- Is it worth the expense in its value to the program?
- Is it important in the general education and the general music education of every child?

It is the purpose of this book to help teachers feel comfortable enough with the new technology to make their own decisions as to how it should be integrated into their programs. It is intended as a guide for using the new technology side by side with what teachers already do. As such, many of the lessons included could easily be carried out with or without synthesizers; these lessons are included here as models for integration.

Yet if the lessons can be taught with or without synthesizers, then why bother with the expense and effort to use them at all? The answer lies in the role of electronic music in society today. Does what we offer appear to be "real music" or is "school music" a different and separate entity? Does our program appear relevant to the outside world? Do our students perceive it as relevant to their world? Can we defend our programs to the layperson? Can we continue to ignore this part of American musical culture and still maintain our credibility?

We need not change what we teach, only how we teach it. Using technological advances in the music classroom does not mean we have to change our priorities. It provides us with the opportunity to give ourselves a face-lift, a new suit of clothes.

There are many ways of knowing the world, and musical understanding is one of these ways. A good music education program must include avenues for increasing an individual's capacity for knowing his or her world. The new technology, in the form of synthesizers and computers, can provide students with opportunities to increase their awareness of their own world views and to manipulate the elements of their musical perceptions such that they can increase their understanding of their own experience.

The first section of this book, Getting Started, examines some available equipment and the teacher education necessary to use it and provides information that will help familiarize teachers with the functions and capabilities of the instruments. The second section presents an overview of a variety of uses in the classroom. The third section, Introducing Synthesizers to Children, offers suggestions for using electronic instruments in all aspects of the music curriculum and provides lesson plans for the teacher's use.

The lessons presented in this book are suggested as guidelines for integrating today's technology into an existing curriculum. Synthesizers can be most useful in the elementary music program for improving performance and listening skills and for nurturing creativity. The lessons in this book are designed to enhance the students' perceptions of and ability to use the basic elements of music: rhythm, melody, harmony, form, dynamics, timbre, and texture. As the students develop an increased understanding of these basic elements, and of their interaction in a musical context, they also expand their capacity to experience the inherent aesthetic value of music. The importance of working within a musical context cannot be overemphasized. Each lesson is either derived from a particular musical composition or designed to help students create their own musical context. Teaching about elements with no musical context is not really teaching music; it is teaching terminology.

Each lesson also includes several different musical experiences that evolve from the three possible means of interaction with music: listening, performing, and creating. Children might be asked to describe their perceptions of a listening experience through movement, iconic representation (diagrams), or verbalization, depending upon their musical maturity. They might perform by singing or playing classroom instruments. Children can create music through both spontaneous, exploratory improvisation and composition (planning the piece to the extent that it can be recalled and reproduced at a later time). These experiences are designed to broaden the students' understanding of the basic concepts and structure of music, which in turn enhances their ability to value music in their lives.

While the units that appear in this book are interrelated, they are not intended to be taught one lesson after another to the exclusion of other musical activities. There must also be a rich assortment of activities and experiences in the general music class that takes into account a variety of learning styles and gives equal attention to listening, performing, and creating. In most cases, the lessons appearing in this book should not be presented on consecutive days. Rather, they should be interspersed throughout the semester alternating with more traditional lessons. A listening and analysis lesson may be scheduled for one class period, and an exercise in small-group composition, using only acoustic instruments, might be scheduled for another. On some days singing, accompanied by a variety of instruments, may be the main experience, while on other days an entire class period may be allotted for synthesizer work. Variety of experience is the key.

Synthesizers can play a part in each of these activities, used side by side with the usual classroom equipment to enhance these experiences.

We are all aware that books about technological advances tend to become outdated quickly, but the practicing teacher can measure future decisions with the basic guidelines presented in this book. A particular piece of hardware or software must be judged according to its potential to enhance our ability to teach what we believe to be important in the music education of our students.

GETTING STARTED

Teachers need only a basic knowledge of synthesizers to use them successfully in the classroom. Electronic instruments are not difficult to understand. While a deeper understanding of synthesizers and of their capabilities is an option open to any music teacher, such an understanding is not essential to successful classroom use of the technology.

Success in the music classroom requires minimal equipment. One can start small and add equipment as the need arises. This enables both the teacher and the students to learn about new hardware as it is acquired. Also, the arrival of a new instrument is exciting—each new unit is itself a motivational force.

The best way for the teacher to attain a basic knowledge of electronic instruments is to learn from someone who knows. Take a good course, if one is available. If it is necessary to rely on books and manuals, try to find one that is written specifically for the equipment to be used. Often, the best manual is not the one provided by the manufacturer. More detailed manuals can be purchased separately. As with computers, the instructions and commands needed to make synthesizers function differ from one brand of equipment to another. It is not difficult, however, to make a transition from one model to another once you understand some of the basic principles.

EQUIPMENT

Synthesizers can either be *programmable* or not. Most students own *nonprogrammable* keyboards. Some manufacturers call their nonprogrammable instruments "keyboards" and their programmable instruments "synthesizers." If the school budget allows, teachers should choose programmable instruments because they provide more options for classroom use.

A synthesizer incorporates a sound source and a computer. In smaller keyboards, available in music stores and department stores, the computers are factory-programmed. They have what are known as *presets*; pressing certain buttons will give the player a menu of preset sounds for the keyboard. On most of the units, another set of buttons will provide preprogrammed accompaniment patterns and built-in *digital drum patterns*. Users can play chord patterns that automatically combine with the drum patterns, and can then add a melody on the higher notes of the keyboard. There is generally a tempo controller and a volume "slider." These, however, are the only controls available to the performer.

Professionals work with a very different caliber of instrument, *programmable* synthesizers. These are much more useful and appropriate for the classroom. They tend to be more costly but are certainly more worthwhile because the design of these instruments gives one access to the internal computer. Programmable synthesizers generally contain a number of preset sounds, and this capability is expandable (through the use of *RAM and ROM cards*, which are similar to computer disks).

One of the more flexible features of these instruments (though not necessarily the most important feature for elementary music class) is that they allow the user to edit the timbre of the sounds they produce. New sounds are created by altering the existing ones.

With *multitimbral* keyboards, sounds can be combined. Eight or more different sounds can be played simultaneously; this flexibility makes them preferable to single-timbre units for classroom use. Classroom usefulness, of course, depends on practicality as well as potential: some instruments are more "user-friendly" than others. The clearer the layout of controls and presentation of instructions, the easier it will be for both the teacher and the children to learn to program the instruments.

If possible, choose a keyboard with *touch-sensitive* keys. This will give the performer greater flexibility and musicality. Some keyboards have as an additional feature, a joystick, a wheel, or other means of altering the sounds during performance without using the program mode.

It is preferable to own a synthesizer that has *MIDI* (Musical Instrument Digital Interface) capabilities. MIDI is an international standard, a computer language, through which most of today's electronic music equipment communicates. MIDI enables one synthesizer to control another. Through MIDI, a keyboard can be connected to a standard computer through an interface. With available software the teacher can set up a combined synthesizer-computer system. In such a system, the computer can function as a sequencer (a device for storing and editing the notes and other commands that go into playing a composition), as a voice editor (a device for altering the sound produced by a synthesizer while bypassing the small function keys on the instrument itself), or even as a typesetter (providing printed versions of students' compositions). One can also purchase a separate hardware sequencer, although the capabilities of these units are generally limited.

Without the aid of a computer, most sophisticated synthesizers can perform some editing and sequencing functions to a lesser degree, but still to a degree that is highly satisfactory for classroom use. The work of professional electronic-music composers and arrangers usually requires the use of an external computer. For the classroom, built-in functions are sufficient.

Other educational software is available for use with a computer and a MIDI-capable synthesizer together. Most of the software on the market today concerns itself with notation skills; there are many note-reading and rhythm-reading programs. There is also a wealth of eartraining software. Some newer composition and music printing programs are available.

Much currently available software, however, does not deal with what elementary classroom music teachers generally teach. And where it does, in many cases, traditional means of instruction may actually prove to be more effective. Synthesizers are most useful in the elementary program when they are integrated with other instruments for live performance. When this is done, they can help teachers meet the goals of improving performance and listening skills and nurturing creativity.

The development of *CD-ROM* may open the door to an exciting new world of possibilities for classroom music through the use of inter-active software. This innovation makes it possible for a computer to send messages to a compact disc player, permitting a student to engage in an interactive listening experience. In such a setup the student can instruct the computer to access specific portions of a high-quality compact disc recording. For example, the student can ask the system to find and play the second theme of a particular piece of music; graphics can also be incorporated. Students can then play that theme as many times as needed to answer analytical questions posed on the computer screen. To date, there are very few of these computer programs available. However, the development of data-organizing software like Hypercard makes it possible for teachers to design their own computer lessons, making them more flexible and better suited to each teacher's individual curriculum and teaching style.

Most synthesizer manufacturers now offer what they call *worksta-tions*, which combine a keyboard controller, synthesizer for drum and other sounds, and a built-in sequencer. These "on-board," or integral, sequencers perform all of the basic functions of computer-based or stand-alone sequencers; that is, they record the pitches played on the synthesizer, allow the user to edit the recorded "score," and play the composition back on command. In some of these instruments, compositions in progress as well as finished works can be stored on a computer disk. On-board sequencers typically lack some of the advanced editing functions available through computer-based sequencing software and may be able to store only relatively short compositions, but these limitations are fairly unimportant for elementary music teachers.

For the music teacher's purposes, a workstation can be a wonderful tool, even though an elementary curriculum is unlikely to call for all of the unit's potential functions. The teacher can use the equipment to create tracks for performance accompaniments, rehearsal purposes, and demonstration purposes. The sequencing capabilities of the instrument can be used for composing, orchestrating, arranging, and transposing. But, as far as the children are concerned, most elementary children don't as yet possess the skills and conceptualization necessary to use a sequencer. Even if they did, the time required to teach sequencing as a part of an ongoing elementary curriculum is prohibitive. Time spent learning to use the equipment could be better spent expanding student ability to hear more in the music of the world. In addition, owning an instrument where all of the equipment is located in one unit rather than in multiple units that can be approached by distinct, small groups of students eliminates one work area in the classroom. A one-unit workstation could accommodate only four or five students who might not even be able to utilize its many capabilities. However, if the budget allows, it would be wise to purchase one workstation that could become part of a total classroom setup.

Although some sophisticated professional keyboards have programmable digital drums, most lower-priced models do not. The school can purchase a separate programmable *digital drum machine*, which is more practical for classroom purposes as it provides an additional work area for students. It, too, comes with some factory presets to which additional manufacturer-programmèd sounds can be added, but it is easy and more rewarding to learn to program your own. A good drum machine provides flexibility and ease of programming, since each instrumental sound can be programmed (and corrected or erased) separately, and the various parts overlaid as you work. A good drum machine also can be played live in performance. It should have *touch-sensitive pads* so that the performer can make accents and dynamic changes.

In some of the newer, less-expensive keyboard models, the internal computer remains inaccessible but the keyboard itself can be converted into a rather limited programmable drum machine. On these models, the keys are often labeled with pictures of percussion instruments. Students can create their own repeating drum patterns, but they must create the entire pattern at once; these units will not allow users to record their ideas in layers.

Most drum machines and professional synthesizers do require external *amplifiers*, and these are generally not included in the purchase price of the instrument. Although a school public address system

8

or a small bass or guitar amplifier can be used temporarily, only a large and good-quality instrument amplifier will permit students to hear the true sounds of the instruments. Since the output level of a synthesizer is not the same as either a microphone level or the line-level output of a tape deck or other home stereo device, the amplifier should be one designed specifically for electronic instruments. Instrument-level output is closer to that of a microphone than it is to line-level signals, so instruments can be plugged into microphone inputs with only a little loss of sound quality. Of course, *headphones* also can be used for individual and small-group work.

To begin to use electronic equipment in a classroom music program, then, the recommended equipment would be:

- *one keyboard* that is programmable, multitimbral, has MIDI capabilities, has touch-sensitive keys, accepts a headphone jack, and accepts ROM or RAM cards
- *one digital drum machine* that is programmable, has MIDI capabilities, has touch-sensitive pads, accepts a headphone jack, and accepts ROM or RAM cards
- *one amplifier* that accepts two or more (for later expansion) input jacks (one from each instrument), and has a built-in speaker.

As budgeting permits, three or four more synthesizers might be purchased. A combination of four keyboards plus one digital drum machine (along with the necessary amplification system) seems to be a practical number for a general music program that attempts to achieve a balance between listening, performing, and creating. When the students engage in small-group work, this provides five workstations, a reasonable number for a typical class of twenty-five students. When students engage in whole-class performance, it will provide enough instruments for between five and nine student accompanists (depending on whether one or two performers play each keyboard). Because some of the other students can play xylophones or acoustic percussion instruments, and the remainder can sing, more keyboards are not really necessary.

When four keyboards are placed side by side across a table or two, the teacher can monitor the students' performances with a quick glance. More keyboards would make this difficult. When students engage in creative activities, it is important to make available a large selection of both acoustic and electronic instruments. We want to provide opportunities for our students to be able to make value judgments as to the appropriateness of the various timbres. Children presented with a choice do not always opt for the electronic sound. This is important: we must allow our students to experience both the joys and the limitations of electronic sound production.

9

If an inexpensive *mixer* can be added to this setup, it will expand the number of synthesizers, drum machines, or other sound sources that can be played through the amplifier at one time. Even some of the smallest keyboards that students own sound wonderful when played through a large amplifier. The poor sound quality of most small keyboards is due in large part to the size of the units' built-in speakers. Simply plug the output from the keyboard into the mixer and the output from the mixer into the amplifier. By doing this, the number of workstations in the classroom can be increased, and more children can participate.

If there is a *tape recorder* in the room, the amplifier line output can be connected directly to the input of the tape deck. The teacher can then make high-quality recordings. Microphones can be added through the mixer to record singers or acoustic instruments. The purchase of a four-track tape recorder can increase the flexibility of the setup for recording and editing, but it is far from being essential in an elementary music classroom.

Since synthesizers are computers, they should be protected from a possible power surge. *Surge protectors* are inexpensive and easy to use in a standard outlet. Many synthesizers can be plugged into one circuit since they do not use much power. Some school districts can install a kind of extension outlet commonly called a "power pole." This pole can be placed anywhere in the room. Cables are run from an existing wall outlet up the wall, across the ceiling, and down through the hollow center of the pole. The pole has several outlets at the bottom. Plugging equipment into this pole makes it possible to place keyboards away from the walls while eliminating the possibility that students might trip over wires that are stretched across the floor.

USING STUDENTS' INSTRUMENTS

Many students own synthesizers that can be easily incorporated into classroom projects to supplement available school instruments. Most students seem to be willing to share their keyboards with their peers. It is wise to have a locking cabinet in the music room for storage of these instruments.

Students can use smaller synthesizers to practice difficult parts, and can then move on to the school's larger keyboards. Students' keyboards can also be connected to a large amplifier for live performance.

Whether it be on school equipment or on their own, using electronic instruments in live performance lifts school morale. Students are very proud of their new capabilities, their performances, and their creations.

USES IN THE CLASSROOM

Students can use synthesizers for accompaniment, composition, and improvisation. Electronic keyboards are wonderful tools for working with basic musical concepts, for skill development and practice, and for studying the properties of sound.

Synthesizers can be played in two ways. Students can use them in live performance as they would an acoustic instrument. They can also play preprogrammed music by receiving a stream of data that represents a list of the musical events that make up a composition through a process known as *sequencing*. Sequencing has become a part of many secondary school programs.

With elementary school students, the most beneficial and appropriate use of synthesizers in the music classroom is as a medium for live performance. Hands-on performance allows more children to participate with less equipment. It also allows for more teacher-guided instruction and supervised skill development. A properly planned, hands-on elementary program helps students develop the skills they will need to work independently in secondary school music laboratories.

Young children are not really impressed with what a sequencer can do. They object to the notion of a machine that will play music for them; they want to create it live every time. To be sure that each child will have many opportunities to do so, most of the large group lessons in this book involve a rotation format in class.

A Word about Rotation:

For many of the activities described in this book, the children play at one instrument, and then while the drum machine continues (and the beat goes on), they rotate to another instrument. The instruments, both electronic and acoustic, are set in a large circle in the middle of the classroom. Each child takes a position at one of the instruments. Most often, two students share each instrument, and the two rotate as a team. Since the electronic instruments usually need to be placed near one another, it is best to specify the number of instruments the children should pass over (as they rotate around the circle) before stopping to play again. For example, picture a circle that contains four keyboards

11

(all placed side by side) and eight assorted barred instruments. There are two children at each position. After playing one portion of the piece, all of the teams move to the right two positions (that is, skipping one instrument and sitting at the next). After six repetitions, every child has played a keyboard twice and a barred instrument four times. Let the drum machine continue as they move and establish a set number of beats that must pass before they begin each repetition. After a while, you can make it the children's responsibility to count the number of beats before they play again. It is a marvelous tool for developing inner hearing.

Through this process of rotation, children learn their various roles through participation in whole activities (as opposed to isolated segments) while working side by side with an adult. The student assumes the role of an apprentice musician and the teacher that of the expert. All of the children are participating in a complete and real musical experience. The piece continues as each child plays his or her part in the musical whole.

This approach leaves the teacher free to work with individuals as they pass around the circle. The teacher can easily stand beside a more experienced child and subtly nudge him or her to a more difficult level. (For example: when the group is learning to play a bass line, it is easy to stand next to a student pianist and, without a word, model the chords that will be needed later on. The student will understand and follow your lead.) It is just as easy to position yourself next to a child who is having trouble in order to lend a silent hand. Because both the music and the student participation are continuous, the individual attention is unobtrusive. Also, if the teacher performs as part of the circle but remains at one keyboard as the students move around, each student will get an opportunity to work side by side with the teacher and to learn by observing the teacher's model. The class can function musically for an extended period of time with no need for the interruption of verbal directions.

TEACHING MUSICAL CONCEPTS

As a way of teaching and reinforcing basic concepts of music, electronic keyboards provide a useful tool with immediate feedback. Texture, timbre, and other concepts can be clearly demonstrated. In hands-on working with these instruments, students gain invaluable knowledge as they alter the fundamental parameters of musical sounds.

Older students who have studied the role of the basic elements of music throughout their early years are generally ready for a more in-depth approach. They are prepared for analysis and synthesis and for study of the ways in which music elements are combined. Synthesizers are a constructive tool for studying and performing sophisticated musical forms like the blues and ground bass.

COMPOSITION

Composition provides an excellent means of teaching and reinforcing abstract musical concepts. Students can learn to deal with the abstract when the teacher provides them with concrete tools. By creating their own music on a synthesizer, students gain personal experience with musical form and structure. Student composers must manipulate all the components of music, which requires the practical application and synthesis of musical concepts.

Composition also serves as an excellent evaluative tool. Students who have been working with a particular musical element or idea through other activities can be asked to use that idea as a basis for creating an original composition. Analysis of that composition by the teacher can provide insight into the level of student comprehension of the idea. These compositions can involve electronic and acoustic instruments. An important part of musical decision-making is choice of timbre as this involves evaluation and judgment on the part of the student.

When children compose original songs, they often enjoy the use of synthesizers to generate accompaniments; synthesizers are both versatile and contemporary-sounding. Synthesizers in the classroom motivate students to be creative. Children working independently (with headphones) can create imaginative compositions inspired by the wealth of interesting timbres available for easy access.

Students can perform compositions live or record them with a standard tape recorder. Working to perfect a live performance is a valid way of developing a young child's musicianship.

OTHER USES

Synthesizers are easily incorporated into improvisatory experiences. For example, students can use the keyboards to establish the underlying chord progression while other players improvise on familiar classroom xylophones. These same children eventually will become competent enough to improvise on the keyboard itself. These activities help to develop musicality and creativity.

In planned as well as improvised settings, older elementary students can use synthesizers to accompany songs. They can play bass lines, ostinatos, chord progressions, fill-ins, and percussion parts in live performance. Electronic instruments also can be used side by side with acoustic classroom instruments.

Electronically created sound effects can be used as introductions to songs and as special effects in class songs, original compositions, in plays and school productions, and to embellish environmental sound pieces. Students learn to consider the appropriateness of a given sound using the higher-level thinking skills of analysis, synthesis, and evaluation.

One or more synthesizers can be used as the basis of a classroom station for independent work and small-group projects. Other stations in the room might include xylophones, Autoharps, recorders, percussion instruments, a piano, or a tape recorder and headphones. Synthesizers are always the favorite station and, because they can be used with headphones, the quietest.

Having children perform live on synthesizers opens up many new possibilities. Keyboards can easily accompany a chorus, add to a band or an orchestra, or be used in a homogeneous, self-contained ensemble. They can generate tremendous excitement and support for the entire school music program.

Performances on electronic instruments can easily be tape-recorded, and children love to hear their own performances on tape. It adds an exciting dimension to the classroom program.

INTRODUCING SYNTHESIZERS TO CHILDREN

The arrival of an electronic instrument in the classroom is an exciting moment. Most elementary students have never seen a sophisticated synthesizer.

Beginning lessons should be experimental. The students will need time to learn how the synthesizer works. You might begin by allowing each child in turn to select one of the preset sounds and then play a few notes. This usually involves selecting two numbers, pressing those buttons, and playing some keys. The sounds are so interesting that children eagerly sit while twenty-five different sounds are played.

Even very young children can operate the synthesizer. When they do, they become familiar with the instrument, thereby gaining an understanding of timbre, pitch, and direction. By taking turns selecting sounds, children are dealing with cause and effect and are also introduced to the rotation method of sharing.

During the first synthesizer lessons, you can demonstrate a few of the more advanced and attractive features such as portamento control, which creates a sliding effect from note to note, and vibrato control. Most keyboard programs include a few sound effect presets like hurricanes, motorcycles, and earthquakes. If the keyboard is multitimbral, demonstrate a combined sound. By now, the class should be familiar with the new instrument and anxious to learn more. The next step depends on the age level of the class.

LESSON PLANS FOR PRIMARY GRADES

In kindergarten through grade 3, electronic instruments can be used as any instrument would be used. Young children can be taught to keep a steady beat on a drum machine or to play a bourdon (repeating tonic/dominant bass pattern) or ostinato on a keyboard. The transition from classroom xylophones and acoustic drums to electronic instruments can be smooth, and children can learn to use them interchangeably. Because of the vast selection of sounds available, synthesizers can appropriately be used to accompany almost any song.

To Accompany a Primary Song:

Many primary level songs can be accompanied by open fifths on a classroom xylophone. For example:

Students can learn to play the same parts on a keyboard. Young children might begin by playing them first on a large xylophone. The movement involved in hitting a xylophone uses gross-motor coordination, while the keyboard involves fine-motor finger dexterity; young children need to experience both. For most the transition seems easy.

Children who can play a steady beat or simple rhythm on an acoustic drum can benefit from playing the same pattern with one finger on the pad (button) of a digital drum machine. Once again, the student learns to execute the pattern with both gross-motor and fine-motor muscles.

Using Sound Effects:

Primary students can experiment with sound effects to embellish songs and projects. In many classrooms, students use acoustic instruments and vocal sounds to embellish songs and stories. Adding electronic sounds can make these lessons even more exciting. You may want to incorporate environmental, vocal, and body sounds for special effects into your lesson plans. The menu of sound effects available on most sophisticated synthesizers provides an exciting addition to projects such as introductions to Halloween songs.

Some teachers use stories and poems to relate or review musical concepts:

- Loud, low pitches: Giants' and monsters' voices.
- Soft, high pitches: Little birds' and mice's voices.

- Melodic contours: Characters climbing up and down.
- Melodic activity: Slow or fast movements of characters.
- Repetitive rhythms: Phrases transferred to instrument parts to help children feel and practice rhythms; for example, "You can't catch me, I'm the Gingerbread Man!"

Before you begin the story, have the children select appropriate sounds for the different characters and motions you will need. By choosing sounds, listening to the sounds critically, and evaluating their appropriateness, students learn to discriminate and categorize. By performing the sounds as the story unfolds, they begin to develop ensemble skills. The resulting story with sound effects is usually an aesthetically pleasing, productive experience for the children. As students continue to grow, these early experiences lay the groundwork for improvisatory mood pieces and the like.

LESSON PLANS FOR
UPPER ELEMENTARY GRADES

Specific instruction in performance practices and in the unique qualities of electronic instruments is more appropriate for grades 4–6. The following lessons offer a good starting point for upper elementary students.

All children should work directly with sounds in music class. Older students, however, can gain a great deal from an introduction to some of the ideas behind the process of synthesis. You may find that a short introduction to the science of sound production will help children grasp the more traditional music-class topic of instrument classification. Synthesis in the music classroom helps students understand the similarities and differences between different classes of instruments.

UNIT 1
Synthesis and Amplification

All instruments have a sound (vibration) source plus some form of amplification. In a synthesizer, the source of vibration is electronic and is controlled by a computer.

Physical Vibration Source

+ Physical Amplifier

= Acoustic Instrument

Physical Vibration Source

+ Electronic Amplifier

= Electric or Electrified Instrument

Electronic Impulse ("vibration") Source

+ Electronic Amplifier

= Electronic Instrument

The synthesizer's computer allows it to mimic different combinations of vibration sources and amplifiers.

It is helpful for children who are going to deal musically with the various aspects of sound to have some understanding of the science of sound. For example, it is useful if they know about vibration and sound waves as well as their amplification. Since science curricula vary from area to area, one can not assume that the students come into the music class with this knowledge.

Students can discover these principles through some simple experiments in the science of sound. If they have had no previous experience with the principle of vibration, strum an Autoharp and have them place their fingers gently on the strings. Then have them lightly place their fingers on their own voice boxes when they speak or sing. In both instances they should feel the buzz of the vibration.

Students can do the two experiments that follow during the same lesson. Have some children take turns with the hanger while others are making the cups. Do not tell the children what the outcome of the experiments should or will be. Do not reveal the purpose of the projects until the end. The mystery is part of the fun.

Lesson 1: Sound Waves and Amplification

Objective:
To help children discover the principles of amplification of a sound.

Materials for Experiment 1:
Each child will need:
> A small paper cup
> A toothpick
> A piece of string 2-3 feet long

You will also need a bowl or pot of water (or a sink in the room).

Procedure for Experiment 1:
1. Give each child one cup, one toothpick, and one piece of string.
2. Poke a hole in the bottom of the cup with the toothpick.
3. Poke the string through the hole.
4. Break the toothpick so that it is short enough to lie flat in the bottom of the cup.
5. Take the end of the string that is inside the cup and tie it around the toothpick (see figure 1). Be certain not to pull the string out of the cup.

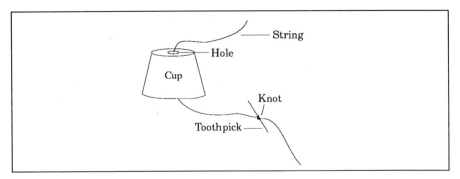

Figure 1.

6. Pull back on the string so that the cup will hang on the string.
7. Wet the string (not the cup) in the bowl or sink of water.
8. Holding the cup in one hand, slide your fingers along the string several times. Warn the students not to put the cup next to their ears. The sound will be surprisingly loud.

The students have made an amplifier!

The string is the sound source (source of the vibration) and the cup has amplified the sound. Explain that sound is vibration. Vibrations cause waves in the air much the same way that waves appear in water when a rock is dropped into it. An amplifier makes those waves grow larger. Larger, "deeper" waves make louder sounds. Students may be interested to know that this instrument, the "Lion's Roar," is used in some folk musics and by some highly respected composers (such as Edgard Varése).

Materials for Experiment 2:
You will need:
      Several wire hangers
      Two pieces of string each 2-3 feet long

Procedure for Experiment 2:
1. Tie a length of string to each end of a wire hanger (see figure 2).
2. Have a student wrap the ends of the strings around his or her index fingers and put their fingers (not the string) in either ear.
3. The student should then swing the end of the hanger so that it will hit something in the room such as the desk or the garbage can.
4. The child will hear the sound like a gong–but everyone else will hear a gentle "clink."

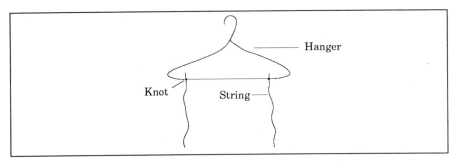

Figure 2.

This experiment shows the role of amplification.

Sound travels through a solid with very little loss of power. Sound travelling through the air loses intensity as it travels. The string carries the vibration through the bones of the fingers directly to the bones of the ear, where it takes on a very different color from the "unamplified" sound.

Lesson 2: Classification of Instruments

Objective:
To discover the differences between acoustic, electronic, and electrically amplified acoustic instruments.

Materials:
For this lesson, you will need:
> Xylophone with removable bars (a metallophone works best)
> Synthesizer
> Amplifier
> Various acoustic instruments (especially stringed instruments)
> An electric guitar (if possible)
> Piece of string about 2 feet long
> Mallet

Procedure:
1. Take one of the bars off the xylophone. Thread a piece of string through one of the holes in the bar. Let it hang free. Hit it with a mallet. It will vibrate, but the sound will be very soft. This demonstrates acoustic vibration.
2. Place the bar back on the xylophone. Hit it again. It will be louder. Ask the students if they know why. Some of them will make the

21

connection to the paper cups used in Lesson 1; they will figure out that the resonating chamber of the xylophone serves as an amplifier. Point out that the size of the resonating chamber of different xylophones is proportional to the size of the bars. Lower pitches produce longer sound waves and therefore require larger chambers for amplification. This demonstrates acoustic amplification.

3. Locate the sound sources and amplifiers on other acoustic instruments. Show students other acoustic instruments. See whether they can identify the sound source and the amplifier. (Stringed instruments are obvious examples.) All acoustic instruments have something that produces a physical vibration, which is then amplified physically (through acoustics). This makes them acoustic instruments.

4. Ask the students whether or not they have seen an electric guitar. Show them a solid-body guitar if possible. Does it have a resonating chamber? When someone strums the strings, is it as loud as an acoustic guitar? Why not? What is missing? It has strings that produce a physical vibration, but it requires an electronic source for amplification. This demonstrates electrical amplification of an acoustic instrument.

An electric guitar is the easiest electrified instrument to understand. Yet any instrument can be electrified by playing it into a microphone and using an amplifier to increase its sound power.

5. Demonstrate the properties of an electronic instrument. Ask the students if they can figure out what vibrates in a synthesizer. They will probably guess that it is the wires, or some variation of that idea. There is no real way for them to discover what vibrates, since it cannot be seen. Briefly explain that the sounds do not originate from vibrations at all. They are the result of a series of electrical impulses similar to turning a light on and off. It is the arrangement of "ons" and "offs" (the "digits" of the synthesizer's digital computer) that creates the different sounds. These digits are translated into electrical vibrations like those carried by the guitar's cord.

6. Demonstrate electronic amplification of an electronic sound. Can a synthesizer play at all without an electronic amplifier? Unplug the connecting cable and invite a student to play the keyboard. Unlike the electric guitar, which has a physical vibration, synthesizers produce no sound when there is no amplifier. Electronic instruments require an electronic sound source and electronic amplification.

7. Allow the students to select a few sounds and experiment with them.

8. For further study, you can explain the term "digital sound." Children who have studied grids in mathematics can understand that a sound wave can be plotted on a grid (see figure 3). The inter-

secting points can be given numbers that can be stored as digital data. Not all students will grasp this, or need to, but it may be worth a few minutes for those who have been exposed to the mathematical ideas involved.

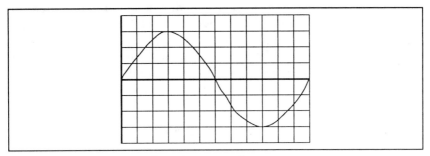

Figure 3. Sound wave plotted on a grid.

UNIT 2
First Performance Experiences

Before attempting these lessons, students need to have had some experience improvising on acoustic instruments. Electronic instruments should supplement an existing program, not replace it. The following activities foster musicianship, listening skills, and creativity. They are also fun.

Using xylophones with removable bars, which are ideal for improvisation, young children can create introductions and codas or interludes between verses of simple songs. Lacking an adult's inhibitions, they will easily fill the space you indicate with their own improvisations.

Older students can improvise entire pieces. For example, set up several xylophones to play a pentatonic scale (or use all of the diatonic bars). Ask the lower-pitched instruments to find a pattern that keeps a beat. The higher-pitched instruments can then play "questions and answers." You and your students can devise many variations of this type of piece.

Older children enjoy and learn a great deal from participating in free improvisation. Set a variety of pitched and nonpitched acoustic instruments in a circle on the floor. Ask the children to sit around the outside of the circle of instruments. One volunteer, or the teacher, can begin. Students may join in or drop out as they choose in this "conversation without words." Encourage the children to listen carefully to one

23

another so that what they play reflects what someone else has played. Suggest that they either answer someone, copy someone, or play something that complements someone else's music. The mood may be maintained or may change suddenly with a solo.

Try to establish a mood beforehand. Ask students to pretend that they have been hired to write a movie score. Relate a short setting or portion of a story. Ask them to describe what they think the background music might sound like. Then begin the improvisation. Don't be discouraged; the first few attempts may be disastrous. It sometimes takes several tries before the students get the idea.

Lesson 1: A Beginning Ensemble Experience

When students first play in an ensemble that includes both electronic and acoustic instruments, they will need to concentrate on keyboard skills. This lesson does not include singing or live percussion. It is designed to give many students a first performance experience on a synthesizer.

Students in any class will have varying levels of familiarity with keyboard instruments. Some may study piano privately or have a piano or synthesizer at home, while others may have no previous experience with a keyboard instrument. It is easy to individualize within the class structure to accommodate these varying levels.

To begin a lesson, choose students who are familiar with the keyboards. Their prior experience will make the introductory moments of the lesson smoother and clearer to the others. Students with the least experience should begin practice on the more familiar xylophones. Once they are comfortable with what they have learned, they can transfer to the keyboard. The class will eventually rotate so that each student has a chance to play everything.

Objective:
To familiarize students with playing a bass line and a parallel chord progression on the keyboard.

On Chalkboard:

		Em	Em			
Dm	Dm			Dm	Dm	
						C C

Equipment:
- Two or more bass xylophones with removable bars (or whatever is available). Remove all bars except C–D–E.

24

- Alto or tenor xylophone with removable bars. Remove all bars except D–F–A–C.
- Alto or tenor xylophone with removable bars. Remove all bars except C–E–G–B–D.
- Keyboard setting that blends well with xylophones such as a piano, electric piano, or vibes.
- Drum machine. Use either preset four-beat pattern or program a "soft rock" beat such as:

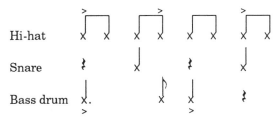

Procedure:

1. Play the progression on the keyboard (four beats to each chord) and sing the bass line with letter names.

   Say: D - - - D - - - E - - - E - - -
          D - - - D - - - C - - - C - - -

   Choose a tempo that is slow enough to give everyone time to think (M.M. ♩ = 96). (If students are more familiar with syllable names or numerals, use do-re-mi or 1-2-3 instead of letter names. Coordinate these lessons with the existing curriculum wherever possible.)
2. Have the class join in singing the bass line.
3. Ask one student to start the drum machine. The class sings the bass line again.
4. Have four students play the bass line on bass xylophones (two to each) along with the drum machine and the teacher playing on the keyboard (see the example on page 26). If possible, set up more xylophones so that more students can play.
5. Explain how to find D on a keyboard. Show that it is located between each set of two black keys.
6. Show the relationship between the xylophone and the keyboard. Allow the students to discover the similarity between C–D–E on the two instruments.
7. Ask a student who plays piano to play the bass line on the lower notes of the keyboard. Add this to the xylophone and drum parts. You should continue to play the chords on the other end of the keyboard.
8. At this point, ask a student who is able to play the chords to do so. The resulting ensemble should have an appealing and pleasant sonority.

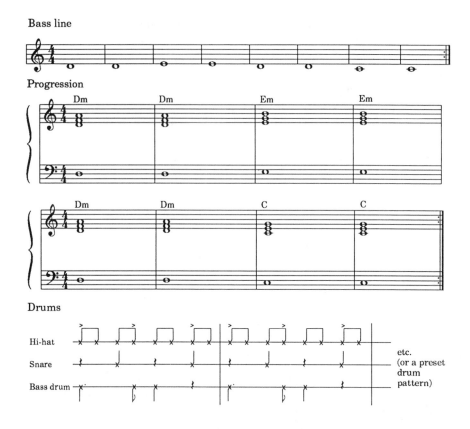

Bass line

Progression

Drums

Lesson 2: Additions to Dm-Em-Dm-C Progression

Objective:
To develop the students' abilities to play a bass line and a parallel chord progression on the keyboard.

Equipment:
Same as previous lesson plus resonator bells.

Procedure:
1. To help children discover what a chord is, ask a nonpianist to come to the keyboard and play any white key. Ask him or her to play that key and its neighboring white key simultaneously. Children will generally conclude that the sound (a second) is not a pleasant or soothing one.

   Instruct the student to skip a key (in either direction) and play the two pitches simultaneously (forming a major or minor third). The class will generally decide that this is a more pleasant sound.

Add a third pitch in the same manner. The students will discover that a combination of skipped keys produces a comfortable and familiar sound.

2. Demonstrate the same idea on a xylophone, which is easier for a large group to observe. Tell the class that this combination of pitches is called a chord. Explain that a chord is: 1) three or more pitches 2) arranged in skips 3) played simultaneously.

3. Model the way a chord is played on the keyboard. Children who have not studied piano often have a difficult time playing chords with correct piano fingering. Suggest several options. First show the correct fingering for piano (1-3-5) using the thumb, middle finger, and pinkie of the right hand. Then present these two alternatives: using the thumb, index finger, and middle finger of the right hand (1-2-3), or, with both hands, using the left index finger, right thumb and index finger (2-1-2).

This might make playing the keyboard less threatening to the novice. As the year progresses, nonpianists often strive to copy the pianists and take great pride in being able to emulate them.

4. Show nonpianists a good way to move from chord to chord. This Dm-Em-Dm-C chord progression is useful because it does not contain large shifts of hand position. Nonpianists can easily be taught to slide their hands from the Dm chord up and back down again, rather than lifting the hand to a more distant chord.

5. Add xylophone soloists. Select new students for the xylophones and keyboard. Turn on the programmed soft rock drum pattern and play. Students should use the xylophone or resonator bells set up for D–F–A–C for improvised solos with the Dm chords, whenever they are played. The C–E–G–B–D setup is for the other two chords. For this part, select a capable student who understands that the C–E–G–B is used for the C chord and the E–G–B–D for the Em chord.

Each soloist fills eight beats with his or her improvisation. The Dm solo is first, then the other student takes over. Since students are playing all of the other parts, the teacher is free to give attention to the soloists. The teacher can actually conduct the solos and cue them. After a few repeats, everything should begin to flow.

6. Rotate instrument parts so that everyone has a chance to play each part. At first, you might prearrange students' instrument assignments. After some practice, the students themselves will quietly move on to a new part or will allow a student who has not yet played to take over. Since the drum machine supplies a constant background and does not stop at the end of the progression, students seem to know that the piece is not yet over. As they finish each part, they tend not to stop and talk about what they have

done, but silently trade instruments and get ready to play again (see "A Word about Rotation," p.11). The following is one possible realization of the progression.

Any solo is acceptable and should be praised. If a team of soloists really listens to one another and plays question-and-answer melody patterns, point this out to the class and praise the musicality of the performance. The goal is for the two players to learn to work as one for each improvisation. A positive, accepting atmosphere will encourage continued improvement and musical growth.

Eventually, students who feel comfortable at the keyboard may be able to perform as soloists improvising chord tones on the synthesizer. Some students may even attempt to incorporate passing tones and other nonchord tones into their improvisations.

Older or more advanced students can try to play chords with the rhythm pattern as follows:

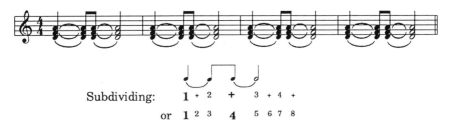

Subdividing: 1 + 2 + 3 + 4 +

or 1 2 3 4   5 6 7 8

Help the students subdivide to eighths; this makes it easier to feel the rhythm pattern. Use whatever counting system you have adopted for your curriculum.

The preset drum pattern can be embellished by a student playing the drum pads live along with the preset. Drum pads are the touch-sensitive buttons through which a digital drum is played and programmed. They are similar to keys on a keyboard but are assigned tone colors rather than pitches. A student might add an occasional handclap, tambourine, or cabaça sound at an appropriate point, such as at the end of each phrase.

Adding Recorders:

If students can play recorders, a recorder melody might be added. Add instruments or music elements one at a time while the players continue to repeat their parts. The piece should always build upward from the drum track and the bass.

Recorder melody

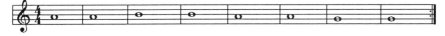

When the piece is finished, and everyone has had a turn, you might ask one student to fade the drum part with the drum machine's volume controller or simply to hit the stop button. You might ask the students to play three C chords as an ending to the final repetition. Then all synthesizer players (including the student in charge of the drum machine) fade their volume controllers together.

The resulting piece should be aesthetically pleasing. The class should function smoothly with little or no interruption in the musical flow. It should prove to be quite rewarding for both the teacher and the students.

This lesson addresses the needs of students at many different skill levels. Some will consider it a challenge to play the bass line on the xylophone, while more advanced students have an opportunity to grow. Although each student takes a turn at each part during the rotation, there should be no pressure on any of them to play their respective parts perfectly. Since they are all part of a single ongoing musical experience, students who have trouble with one part or another tend to feel a part of the experience anyway. Unless students are singled out, they will continue around the circle and improve with practice, experience, and subtle guidance from the teacher. More advanced students generally feel free to improvise or expand their parts on their own.

Lesson 3: Playing a Blues Progression

This lesson would logically follow a series of lessons on the blues. As one of the only forms of music originating in America, the blues is an integral part of our heritage.

Children can listen to a simple blues song and sing its bass line. They can discover that a typical blues consists of twelve measures, four beats to a measure, following the progression:

I	I	I	I
IV	IV	I	I
V	IV	I	I

They can hear that a blues song usually has three lines of lyrics, and that the first two lines are often the same.

Students can play blues bass lines on xylophones and compose their own blues song lyrics with titles like "The Sixth-grade Blues." Many grade five and six textbook series contain lessons on the blues and provide both listening and singing material. As a final lesson, students can learn to improvise blues solos using xylophones and synthesizers.

Objective:
To use what we have learned to play a blues progression on synthesizers.

Materials:
For this lesson, you will need:
 At least one keyboard
 Drum machine
 Amplifier
 Various larger xylophones with removable bars; remove all bars
  except C–F–G–C–F–G.
 Small xylophones or resonator bells set up for each chord; remove
  all bars except C–E–G–C–E (C chord), F–A–C–F (F chord),
  and D–F–G–B–D–F (G₇ chord).

Procedure:
1. Select or program a drum pattern that has a swing style rhythm ($^{12}_{8}$).
2. Ask the students to sing a blues bass line in the key of C:

    C C C C
    F F C C
    G F C C

3. Have several students play the bass line on xylophones. (Two to an instrument; there are two sets of C–F–G on most xylophones.)
4. One or more students play the bass line on the keyboard. (If the keyboard is multitimbral, set the lower notes to a good pizzicato string sound.)
5. Students who are capable of doing so can add chords (sustained for four beats each) on the upper keyboard notes. (If you have the option, set the synthesizers to a piano sound.)
6. Soloists can improvise on chord tones in the appropriate places, as in the previous lesson, using resonator bells or xylophones.
7. If the students have previously written lyrics for blues songs, try alternating one chorus of instrumental improvisation and one of sung blues. The bass line and chords should continue throughout. The soloists stop when the song is finished.

UNIT 3
Synthesizers in Work Stations

   Work stations or learning centers can be an exciting addition to the music classroom. They can be permanent or temporary, depending on the amount of space and equipment available. In practice, the class is divided into groups that circulate from station to station, taking on challenge after challenge. With proper classroom management and well-designed lesson plans, work stations can open many possibilities for both electronic and acoustic instruments.

31

In a large, well-equipped classroom, four or five stations can be set up around the room. The equipment can be left on tables or shelves ready for use, while large-group instruction can take place in the center of the room. In a small room, or in a school where all the equipment is usually in use, stations can be set up quickly as needed. This format can be used with or without electronic equipment, and stations can contain whatever equipment is available.

Autoharp Station:

There might be an Autoharp station with one or two instruments, picks, and a set of instructions. The instructions might contain a song with chord symbols written above the lyrics in the appropriate places. The children at that station would take turns pressing the buttons and strumming, practicing until they could play the song well.

Xylophone Station:

Students at this station might or might not have an assignment related to the song presented at the Autoharp station. This would depend on the goal for the lesson. These students could be asked to learn to play a bass line, simple melody, or ostinato that will later relate to the other instrument parts.

Percussion Station:

This station contains acoustic percussion instruments. These students might be asked to learn a rhythm pattern for the same song or they might have an unrelated assignment. Give these students the option of playing softly or using their hands to play. (If misused or abused, these instruments could make it difficult for other children to hear.)

Listening Station:

If the room has a cassette tape player and a listening station that takes several headphones, several students can be given a cassette tape with projects or listening assignments. Again, these may or may not be related to the other assignments.

Synthesizer Station:

There might be one synthesizer station or several, depending on the availability of equipment. It is often practical to build one station around the drum machine. The students at the drum machine might create and record a drum track for a song to be performed. A keyboard at another station allows students to practice a specific chord progression. (More proficient students would try the chords; others might simply play the bass line.) Try to assign at least one pianist to each group, so that as they rotate, each station will have a student familiar with the keyboard.

The synthesizer station may have instructions for basic programming. In this case, students might be asked to call up a given sound and find the correct control to alter its pitch, timbre, or duration. Work stations make this kind of hands-on work possible in a class because everyone else is busy.

Lesson 1: Rehearsal of a Class Song in Stations

Objectives:
To review chords and bass lines.
To use what has been learned about them to accompany a class song.
To practice the parts of a class song independently in stations.

Materials:
You will need:
> Any simple song with few chords (for example, I, IV, V7)
> Three stations in the classroom:
> Keyboard station (could include a piano or student-owned keyboards)
> Xylophone station (various barred instruments set up with the notes of the bass line)
> Autoharp station (two or three Autoharps)

On Chalkboard:
Write the chord progression for the song, for example:

$$\begin{array}{cccc} G & G & G & G \\ C & C & G & G \\ D7 & D7 & G & G \end{array}$$

Indicate the number of beats each chord will last (in this case, one chord per measure).

Procedure:
(This lesson usually takes two class periods.)
1. In the first class, explain what is to be done in each station.
   Autoharps: Students will take turns practicing the chords for the song, either in pairs (one pressing the buttons while the other strums) or each playing an instrument.
   Xylophones: Students will take turns learning to play the bass line of the song.
   Keyboards: Some children will play only the bass line on the keyboard. Some will want to play the chords. They should practice in

    teams, with a chord player and bass line player sharing one key-
board.
2. After explaining the assignment for each station, divide the class
into groups and begin work in the stations. Set a reasonable time
limit (generally ten minutes) for each group at each station. Groups
should consist of children of various skill levels so that one student
can help another, if necessary. When time is up, turn off the lights
to signal for them to stop work. Each group moves on to a new station at the same time.
3. Generally, you will need to continue this rotation into a second class
period in order for all students to have an opportunity to work in all
stations.
4. At the end of the second class, perform the song as a large group.
Ask several students to play each part while the others sing. In
future classes, different students will try different parts once they
have practiced and learned them.
5. If you like, add an appropriate drum track or acoustic percussion
part, or a combination of the two.

Lesson 2: Halloween Sound Effects Pieces

Objectives:
To create an effective montage of electronic and acoustic sounds.
To select the sounds, arrange them, and plan a format that will achieve
    the desired effect.

Materials:
Work stations equipped with a variety of electronic and acoustic instruments.

Procedure:
1. Have the class divide into groups of four to six students.
2. For each group the task is to create a piece of music using the available instruments. The piece should have a scary sound to it.
Children may make up a Halloween story and use that as a basis
for their piece, or the piece may consist of a series of sounds of their
choosing.
3. Each group should spend five minutes at each station searching for
sounds. As they move from station to station, students should keep
track of their choices on paper.
4. Once the groups have selected sounds at each station, they should
meet for five or ten minutes with no instruments, discuss their col-
lection of sounds, and formulate a plan. Remind them that the best

scary music has different dynamic levels and many textures; it is sometimes the sudden changes that make the music frightening.

5. At the end of the class, or during the next class, each group can perform its piece. The groups will require a short time to assemble and set up their instruments.

6. Finished pieces should not be evaluated or compared to one another; but an exercise of this nature has limited educational value if it has no follow-up. It is in the analysis of one another's work that children begin to understand the synthesis of musical ideas into an expressive whole. Each piece should be discussed by the students for its own strong points and unique character. The discussion that follows the performance of a student's work must always be positive and constructive to encourage future creativity.

Lesson 3: Simple Programming

Children need to have hands-on experience to learn to use the functions of a synthesizer or to learn to vary the parameters of a given sound. Students can learn to select a sound and then call up the appropriate parameter to change it. They can learn to make these changes, "write" the changed sound to the synthesizer's computer memory, and name the sound. They can also learn to split the keyboard, shift the octave, and use any of the synthesizer's functions—so long as instructions are clear.

The actual steps that the students will have to follow to edit sounds will vary from synthesizer to synthesizer. Also, the manuals that accompany synthesizers may be far from clear and are certainly not written with the requirements of elementary music curricula in mind. You will, then, probably have to spend some time familiarizing yourself with the equipment and writing out coherent, logical instructions for the students' use.

In your instructions, ask each child in the group to take responsibility for one step. Once the group has established the new sound, have them use it for some purpose. Then reload the synthesizer with the original sound so that the next group can begin again. The children are simply learning the process of programming the synthesizer at this stage. You need not ask them to produce a complete composition around each sound.

Work stations offer a good format for introducing a new programming experience. In order to manage a large group, provide alternative assignments for the remainder of the class. If there are enough keyboards for each station, you could provide duplicate or varying programming assignments. If only one keyboard is available, the remaining stations would contain unrelated assignments for other types of instruments. The assignments should take as much time as the programming stations will take.

Objectives:
Whichever programming skill you choose to teach:
To learn to change the properties of a sound in order to create a new sound, *or*
To learn to split and revoice the keyboard, *or*
To learn to record a drum pattern.

Materials:
Keyboard station
Digital drum station
Xylophone station (soprano, alto, tenor, and bass xylophones or whatever is appropriate for your lesson)
Percussion station (conga drum, claves, and maracas, or whatever is appropriate for your lesson)

Sample Procedure:
Keyboard Station: [1]
Specify that the students should read through all of the instructions before beginning, and that they should be sure they understand them. If they don't, they should ask for help. Each member of the group will perform one step of the instructions.

Instructions:
1. Call up a sound by selecting a two-digit number.
2. Press the FUNCTION button.
3. Use the VALUE slider or the UP/DOWN buttons to change the pitch of the sound. Play the sound on the keyboard while you are altering the pitch. Stop when you are happy with the sound you have made.
4. Use the CURSOR button to move the cursor under OSCILLATOR 2.
5. Alter the pitch of the sound as you did before.
6. When you have a sound that you like, each member of the group should take a turn playing it on the keyboard.
7. When you are finished, raise your hands. We will all stop to share your new sound.

---

1. In this example, students altered the parameters of a given sound using a KORG 707 Performing Synthesizer. The teacher would need to alter the commands if using a different brand of synthesizer.

8. Press any two-digit number. Press your original number. The sound you created should be gone, and the original sound should have returned.

Digital Drum Station: [2]
Specify that the students should read through all of the instructions before beginning, and that they should be sure they understand them. If they don't, they should ask for help. Each member of the group will perform one step of the instructions.

Instructions:
1. In column 1 (Pattern Play/Record), press F-7 (Tempo).
2. Enter the number 100. The tempo will now be 100 beats per minute.
3. In column 1, press F-1.
4. Select Pattern #53. It is a blank track.
5. Press START button. You should hear a metronome. If you don't, move the DATA slider until you do.
6. Make up a BASS DRUM part that fits with the metronome beat. Keep it simple.
7. When you are ready, press STOP. Hold the RECORD button down and press START again.
8. Play one measure of your bass part with the metronome.
9. Stop and listen. You should hear the bass part playing continually.
10. Press STOP. Go back to step six and add another instrument part.
11. Keep going until you have recorded four parts.
12. When you are ready, raise your hands. We will all stop to share your drum track. Then I will show you how to erase it for the next group.

Creating the lessons for these work stations can be time-consuming. However, they are far from one-period lessons; each group might require as much as twenty minutes at each station.

The teacher can ask the class to work in stations for one part of the class, and to come together for some large-group singing during the remaining class time. Lessons such as these are self-motivating. The children come into the classroom eager to pick up where they left off at the end of the previous lesson.

---

2. In this example, students learn to record a drum pattern on a KORG DDD-1 Dynamic Digital Drum. Alter instructions as needed for other hardware.

UNIT 4
Ground Bass

Lesson 1: What Is a Ground Bass?

This lesson incorporates listening, analyzing, performing, and in its later stages, composing and improvising. It is intended as an example of how working with synthesizers can enhance all aspects of a classroom music curriculum, and in any classroom.

Objective:
To understand the way in which a ground bass can generate a piece of music.

Materials:
For this lesson, you will need:

Recording of Johann Pachelbel's "Canon in D"

Five or six xylophones set up in various parts of the room with all notes removed except D, F#, G, A, B, and D. Station three or four students at each instrument. (Larger, lower-pitched instruments are preferable.)

On Chalkboard:

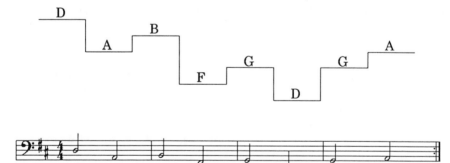

Procedure:
1. Ask the students, "When you build a house, what is the first thing you need to do?" (Make a foundation or basement.) Explain that the foundation supports the house; the house is built on top of it.

Continue with this explanation:

Some musical compositions are also written from the bottom up. The foundation is written first. The rest of the piece is constructed to build upon the foundation. The foundation can be a bass line, similar to those you have been playing on keyboards and xylophones. This bass line is sometimes called a *ground bass*.

2. Ask the class to sing the bass line that is written on the board as you play it.
3. Select several students to play the bass line on the xylophones as the class sings the letter names.
4. Set up a rotation, if possible, so that each student will be able to play the bass line (along with the recording) for two of the variations and then sit down. The change must be smooth since the recording does not stop. The tempo is slow enough for children to make the transition from one player to another easily.
5. Play the recording. Point to the letters on the board to coincide with the bass line of the recording.
6. Each group of students plays two variations and then hands the mallets to the students taking over or moves aside to make room at the keyboard. There should be enough music for each student to have an opportunity to play. Although it is generally not a good idea to ask children to play instruments along with a recording, in this case, it helps them to focus on the ground bass and to understand the construction of the piece. The children should play softly.
7. Students are generally surprised that such a long and complex piece was created from one single bass line.

Lesson 2: Creating a Bass Line

Objective:
To create a piece of music on a ground bass using previous knowledge of chords, creating a bass line, and improvising a melody from a chord.

Materials:
Seven or eight diatonic xylophones stationed around the room. (This lesson in the series does not use synthesizers.)

Procedure:
1. In groups, or as individuals, students will create a ground bass that will serve as a basis for a class composition.
2. Working on any xylophone, a student or group can create a bass line using the following guidelines:
   a. The bass line should be short (five to eight notes in length).
   b. The rhythm should be simple and consistent (e.g. all half notes).

    c. The bass line should be in the key of C because these are diatonic xylophones.

    d. The bass line should therefore end on the home tone, C.

3. After having played the Pachelbel "Canon," the children should have a sense of what they are about to do. They generally tend to play long sustained tones. Many will probably choose to use "acceptable" harmonic structures without really knowing why. Children generally try to emulate the sonorities they have just heard in the recording and choose to accept the most similar sound as the one they like.

4. Ask each student or group to play the bass line for the class.

5. Have students vote to select one bass line that will serve as the foundation of a class composition. (It is sometimes better to narrow the field to the most feasible alternatives and then let the students vote. Students can understand that some bass lines will present fewer problems and make the class assignment easier.)

Lesson 3: Selecting Chords for the Piece

Objective:
To work as a class to select chords (harmonic structure) for a ground bass composition.

Materials:
For this lesson, you will need:
    Chalkboard
    Keyboard instrument (piano or synthesizer)
    Worksheet (optional)

Procedure:
1. The teacher should write the bass line selected in Lesson 2 on the board in both notes and letter names.

2. Distribute the worksheet. The worksheet for each class will contain a different progression, depending on which one was selected in the previous class. Students will fill in some of the answers from the board and some on their own. The worksheet provides space for students to write the finished progression. Students may take it home to practice on an instrument if they own one.

3. Show students that one pitch can fit with each of three different chords (as the root, third, or fifth, although you may choose not to use this terminology). They have learned previously that chords are formed by skips. They know how to spell them from the bottom up (for example C–E–G for a C chord). Show that the pitch C can be part of either a C chord, an Am chord, or an F chord:

```
G
E       E
C       C       C
        A       A
                F
```

Ask the children to figure out what three chords would have the pitch G in common. (Use diatonic pitches only.) At this point, it might be better to say "a kind of A chord" or "a kind of D chord." You might not want to get involved with major and minor unless the students are already familiar with modality.

4. Once they have the idea, ask students to figure out the three possible chords that will fit with each note of their bass line.
5. The teacher can then play some possible combinations. Allow students to select the chord progression by voting on which one appeals to them most.
6. Write the finished product on the board.

Ground Bass Worksheet:

This is the bass line your classmates composed:

C   F   D   G

What chords would work with the first bass note?

```
 G
 E       E
 C       C       C
         A       A
                 F
```

What chords would work with F in the bass?

```
___
      ___
 F       F       F

___     ___
                ___
```

What chords would work with D and what chords would work with G?

```
     ___                      ___
___     ___                ___     ___
 D       D       D          G       G       G
___     ___                ___     ___
        ___                        ___
```

41

Continue with the following explanation: Notice that G and D share a common chord. So do C and F. We might want to consider this in our choice. It might sound good to maintain a chord over two bass notes. It might not. Let's listen.

Then, play various combinations of the suggested chords with the bass line on the piano. Select no more than three possibilities. (Students will not be able to remember the different sonorities.) Allow them to vote on the progression they prefer.

Write out the finished version and ask students to copy it onto their worksheet.

Lesson 4: Composing the Piece

Objective:
To work as a class to compose variations on a previously written ground bass.

Materials:
The class will need:
>Xylophones set up to play the previously composed bass line
>One or more keyboards for bass and chords
>Resonator bells or smaller xylophones for solos
>Completed worksheet

Procedure:
1. Write progression and bass line on the board. They are also on the worksheet.
2. Students should take a few minutes to practice playing the bass line and chords.
3. Now, orchestrate the piece. Some options might be:
    a. A student-composed or preset drum pattern
    b. Several keyboards
    c. Various xylophones, set up with notes for bass line
    d. Resonator bells (three for each chord)
4. Start the drum machine. When ready, add a solo bass line on a keyboard set to a bass sound. (Or have one of the string bass players bring his or her bass to class.) On the next repeat, add the remaining bass line players (xylophones in any register). On the following repeat, add the players who are sustaining chords (on keyboards, piano, guitar, and Autoharps). Next, cue the soloists on the tone bells. They will improvise when their chord is played, taking turns as the piece progresses. Some of the keyboard players will be able to improvise using the chord tones on the synthesizer. Of course, you

will want to encourage the keyboard players to use sounds that they have programmed to be especially appropriate for the composition.

As they did with the Pachelbel "Canon" (Unit 4, Lesson 1), the students quietly rotate without interrupting the flow of the music. In this way, they get a chance to play the bass line, chords, and improvised melody. The resulting piece should sound quite impressive, although different every time since the melodies are improvised and the tone colors may change with shifts among synthesizer players.

UNIT 5
Working with a Drum Machine

A programmable drum synthesizer or drum machine can add many dimensions to a music classroom. Students can use the preset drum patterns, play along with preset patterns, and learn to program their own patterns. The drum settings on many of the newer keyboards can function in much the same way.

Lesson 1: Using the Preset Patterns

Objective:
To become familiar with the functions of a drum machine.

Materials:
You will need to have access to:
>   Programmable drum machine
>   Amplifier or headset

Procedure:
1. Ask one student to select a pattern by pressing the appropriate number combination.
2. Press the START button. The pattern will begin to play.
3. On many models, the next pattern number can be entered without pressing STOP. The pattern will automatically change at the start of the next complete measure.
4. As different students take their turns selecting patterns, try some of the other functions. If there is a TAP TEMPO controller or other means of live tempo control, allow students to alter the speed of the selected pattern. If the drum machine has an internal metronome, show the students how to change the tempo by selecting the number of beats per minute.

5. If the drum machine has drum pads for live performance, show the students where they are and how to play them. Typically, each pad can be assigned to the sound of a different percussion instrument. If the pads are touch-sensitive, demonstrate the different dynamic levels that are possible. (Drum machines are percussion instruments. The pads are intended to be hit and not just pressed.)

Lesson 2: Playing Drum Machine Live with Preset Patterns

Objectives:
To use the drum machine to embellish preset drum pattern.
To learn to transfer rhythm skills from gross motor (acoustic drum) to fine motor (hitting a button) motion.

Materials:
Same as previous lesson.

On Chalkboard:

1	2	3	4	5	6	7	8
1		3		5		7	
	2		4		6		8
		3				7	
1							8
					6	7	
	2	3			6	7	
1					6	7	8

Procedure:
1. Select a drum pattern that moves in $\frac{4}{4}$ time. Find one that has a steady and obvious eighth-note pulse.
2. Set the tempo to a moderate speed (M.M. $\quarternote$ = 100).
3. Ask the students to chant: "1,2,3,4,5,6,7,8" (subdivided eighth notes).
4. Now ask them to chant only the "1,3,5,7." Have students clap those numbers. They are now clapping the steady beat of the $\frac{4}{4}$ measure.

(Sometimes it helps to chant "1,2,3,4,5,6,7,8" while clapping on 1,3,5, and 7.

5. Continue chanting eight beats, feeling subdivided eighths, and clapping the various patterns written on the board.

6. When they are ready, ask some students to select an instrument pad on the drum machine. Have them play only the numbers corresponding to the desired rhythm pattern. For example, have a student play only beats 6 and 7 on a cowbell pad, or cabaça pad.

7. Try several rhythm patterns.

8. Show the students how to accent their rhythms by controlling how hard they hit the pads. Starting on a weak beat and accenting a strong beat (like 2,3...6,7) gives students a good feel for the style.

Lesson 3: Playing Live Fill-Ins in Songs

Objective:
To use the drum machine to embellish the performance of a song.

Materials:
Same as previous lesson, plus a class song (in this case, an original song written by a fourth-grade class).

Procedure:
1. Once students are comfortable and proficient at playing simple rhythm patterns on the drum pads, the drum machine can be used to embellish songs as you would any acoustic percussion instrument.

2. The easiest place for an added drum part is at the end of a phrase.

3. A fourth grade class that had written a song about wearing braces used the drum machine to play a fill-in at the end of each line.

4. "Peanut butter brittle getting stuck in my teeth.
(COWBELL: ♪|♩)
Gum and chewy caramel get stuck beneath. (CABAÇA: ♪|♩)
Can't chew gum. (WOODBLOCK: ♪|♩)
That's no fun. (WOODBLOCK: ♪|♩)
Shiny silver braces give me so much grief." (TAMBOURINE: ♪|♩)

Acoustic percussion instruments could also be used. Allow the students to choose. One interesting aspect of using acoustic and electronic instruments side by side in the classroom is that students develop criteria for selecting one or the other. They often try a digital instrument, listen, evaluate, and then opt for its acoustic version. In a world that is rapidly moving away from acoustic instruments, it is important for future generations to know that they do have a choice, and they must have the knowledge to make that choice.

Lesson 4: Recording a Drum Pattern

Objective:
To learn the process of creating a drum pattern.

Materials:
>   Programmable drum machine with a built-in sequencer
>   Amplifier or headset

Procedure:
1. Find a blank track, or erase a track you will not need.
2. Set the metronome at a relatively slow tempo (M.M. ♩ = 90). The tempo can be increased later.
3. It is easiest to begin in $\frac{4}{4}$ time.
4. Turn on the audible metronome (click track) if you have one.
5. The teacher should enter a basic pattern like the following on the bass drum or another low-pitched instrument:

$$\frac{4}{4} \quad \overset{.}{\downarrow}_> \quad \overset{}{\downarrow}\!\!\flat \quad \downarrow_> \quad \text{\textquotedblright}$$

6. Ask each student to add one sound where he or she would like it to fit. As many as ten to fifteen students can enter sound on one track. Turn the RECORD feature off and allow the student to practice playing the sound he or she wants along with the teacher's basic pattern. Have the student record the part when ready. It is best to accept just about anything at this point. Once several different rhythms have been added by students, the finished product will sound good. If a student is really unhappy with the recording, erase only that instrument part and have the student enter it again.
7. Once the pattern has been created, turn off the click track and have some fun with it.
   a. Have the class stand and move to the beat.
   b. Isolate one particular rhythm pattern or instrument sound, and have the class move in response to it.
   c. Divide the class into groups. One can move to the beat, one to the tambourine part, and one to the cowbell, for example.
   d. Vary the tempo.

These kinds of activities help students develop discrimination skills. Students can learn to program their own drum tracks in small

groups or as an individual project. Most fifth and sixth graders can program a good rhythm pattern independently.

It is important that the instructions (tailored to the individual
demands of your drum machine) are clear, and listed nearby. Make sure
they know what they will need to do to practice their patterns, to record
them, and to erase errors.

Most drum machines have a "quantizing" function that will allow
the computer to correct a less-than-perfect rhythm pattern. But rather
than use this function, have the students erase and redo their tracks
perfecting them as they go. In this way they learn to perform their
rhythm patterns accurately and are motivated to improve their skills.

MORE IDEAS FOR INTERMEDIATE LESSONS

Playing Fill-Ins and Introductions of Popular Songs

Many of today's popular songs have repetitive ostinatos or a particular melodic pattern that appears as an introduction, as a coda, and
between verses. This is because most of the songs are recorded one
track at a time with electronic instruments. In professional recordings,
a sequencer plays these patterns again and again.

In a classroom, this repetition gives the teacher an excellent
opportunity for live student performance. The students can learn the
particular pattern for a song on keyboards, piano, or xylophones. They
can then rotate during a performance of the song, each playing the pattern at an appropriate place on either keyboard or xylophone. The rest
of the class sings. The resulting performance has an air of authenticity
to the children because they are playing the instruments that they hear
used in the recording.

Use in School Performances

Electronic sounds and sound effects enhance any school show or
play. Programmed drum tracks can enliven a production number when
no student drummer has the skills to do so. Teachers can learn to
sequence tracks for musical productions that would have been played
on the piano. This frees them to direct or choreograph. Synthesizers are
easily portable so that outdoor performances are no longer a problem.
In short, the whole school will benefit from this addition to the music
department.

A Student Synthesizer Ensemble

A synthesizer ensemble can be a legitimate performing group in
your school. The ensemble can perform on its own or accompany a

school chorus. Some of the students can play chords, some can play the bass line, and pianists can easily play the melody. Some can play ostinatos or fill-ins.

Synthesizer ensembles can play classical music as well as popular music. Recorder ensemble music can be easily adapted for synthesizers. Each instrument can be set to an appropriate timbre setting as soprano, alto, tenor, or bass.

Children can learn to play very musically on a synthesizer. With good technique it is more like playing a wind instrument or singing than it is like playing a piano. When you lean into a touch-sensitive keyboard, it can make swells, even after the key has been depressed.

Going One Step Further

At this point, upper elementary students have had experience playing bass lines, chord progressions, and melodies. If you have used the sequencer, or sequenced drum tracks in earlier lessons, they have been introduced to the concept of this device. At any rate, they have the basic music skills they need to use a sequencer. It is possible at this point to teach a lesson in composing with electronic instruments and a sequencer.

Either a hardware sequencer, an on-board unit, or software sequencing program could be used. Unless you have an on-board unit, you will need a MIDI set-up of some sort and a bit more knowledge and training on the part of the teacher. (For information on MIDI and equipment, refer to the Getting Started section of this book.)

Sequencers store parts of a composition on "tracks." Just as a multitrack tape recorder might be used to store the instrumental sounds specified by each line of a score on one track, sequencers can conveniently record each voice or part of a composition separately.

Students would begin by creating a bass line and entering that data into the sequencer. They would then decide on appropriate chords and enter them on another track. They could add a drum track. At this point, the sequencer could play back the entire background portion of the piece through the synthesizers. Now, one could either record the melody or add live improvisation on xylophones or additional keyboards.

Some teachers encourage elementary students to create sequences by using "step-entry." In this process, the composer enters a musical line one pitch at a time. The rhythm is then programmed separately. Alternatively, parts that have been entered "in real time," but imperfectly, can be edited to make them correct. One editing function supplied by many sequencers is "quantization." In this process, the composer tells the sequencer to correct the rhythms with which notes were played. He or she determines whether the sequencer will quantize to the nearest quarter, eighth, sixteenth, or other duration. The result is a rhythmically perfect track—as long as the part was originally played with some pretense to accuracy. If the original performance was off by too much, the sequencer may quantize the music incorrectly, leading to results that are both frustrating and funny. The student does not develop *musical skills* in doing this, but develops *programming skills*. It can be an exciting extracurricular project, but it does not really belong in a good elementary music program.

Students generally have negative reactions to the idea that a sequencer or computer plays the keyboards for them. Children enjoy live performance and prefer to be participants. Also, elementary students lack the patience and skills required to create good-quality sound tracks, as well as the desire to cultivate them.

It is preferable, therefore, for children in the elementary classroom to practice their skills in live performance. While sequencing is interesting to some students, it is a time-consuming process to teach that takes time away from other aspects of the curriculum.

SOME FINAL NOTES

Electronic instruments can be a part of almost every aspect of the music curriculum; their very presence adds an extra measure of excitement. Through experiences with synthesizers, children can acquire the skills and knowledge they will need to become intelligent and selective consumers of music as adults. They develop an understanding of the music of their own culture, which can be used as a springboard for developing an understanding of all music.

It is important that children be allowed to develop as musicians within their own musical culture. "School music" and "real music" should not be viewed by children as two separate entities. The music classroom takes on a whole new image when children are given an opportunity to work with sounds with which they are familiar. By integrating synthesizers into a curriculum designed to teach about all music, students are given the opportunity to work with the tools of their own culture. Using these tools, children can learn to understand and manipulate the structural aspects common to all music, but they must begin with what is familiar.

When they are allowed to learn in this fashion, they gradually widen their circle of understanding of music and begin to accept and understand all styles and forms of music. The motivational aspects of using tools of the children's own culture are also highly visible; the children cannot wait for their turns at the synthesizers. The instruments become a central force in the classroom and in the school and can serve to bring an exciting and important dimension to every school music program.

RESOURCES

With the multitude of materials, equipment, and services available, newcomers to electronic music have many decisions to make. Those with limited expertise sometimes find these decisions difficult enough to deter any interest at all.

This list of resources is by no means intended as a complete listing of what is available; neither does it constitute endorsements of particular equipment or services. It is merely a suggestion of good places to begin. In contacting synthesizer companies I found that several have established special programs and options for educators. These listings are intended to inform teachers about these special programs.

EQUIPMENT

Alesis, 3630 Holdredge Avenue, Los Angeles, CA 90016, telephone 800-525-3747; 213-467-8000.
> Quarterly newsletter, *First Reflection.* Customer service division.

Casio Inc., 570 Mt. Pleasant Avenue, PO Box 7000, Dover, NJ 07801, telephone 201-361-5400.

E-mu Systems, Inc., PO Box 660015, Scotts Valley, CA 95067-0015, telephone 408-438-1921.

Ensoniq, 155 Great Valley Parkway, Malvern PA 19355, telephone 215-647-3930.

Kawai America Corporation, Kawai Education Program, PO Box 30772, Long Beach, CA 90853, telephone 800-456-1231; 310-439-3592. Contact Dr. George Shaw, Director of Education Department, or Deana Gordon, Project Manager.
> The Kawai Education Foundation Matching Grants Program will help fund the purchase of equipment and then provide

training, technical support, videos, teachers' guides, seminars, and support systems for participating teachers. Also available are loan and lease programs, a newsletter: *Kawai Music Educators Journal*, books, audio tapes and interactive training software, and the Kawai Education Bulletin Board System (on-line technical support, question and answer forums, and software through an on-line bulletin board that can be accessed through your own computer and modem).

Korg USA, Inc., 89 Frost Street, Westbury, New York, NY 11590, telephone 800-645-3188; 516-333-9100. Contact Lee Whitmore, Educational Director.

Available resources are an educators' newsletter, and a user support system that gives help and answers questions via telephone conference.

Roland Corporation US, 7200 Dominion Circle, Los Angeles, CA 90040-3696, telephone 213-685-5141. Contact Larry Harms, Ext. 303 or Joyce Carden, Ext. 304.

There is a free magazine, *Roland Keyboard Educator*, and other publications and software for teachers. Purchase assistance includes an educator discount, one-year free financing for independent studios, and leasing from 1 to 5 years. Also workshops, and educators on staff for assistance.

Yamaha Music Corporation, 6600 Orangethorpe Avenue, Buena Park, CA 90622, telephone 800-336-6874; 714-522-9011. Contact Karen Ellis, Music Education Division.

Offers teacher training through regional seminars; for those participating in training there is a newsletter, *Crescendo*. Some curricular materials are available to guide group instruction. Workshops and clinics can also be arranged.

SUPPORT SERVICES

Alexander Publishing, 3537 Old Conejo Road, Suite 101, Newberry Park, CA 91320, telephone 800-633-1123; 805-499-6200. Contact Peter Alexander.

They have manuals for all brands of keyboards that are often simpler and clearer than manufacturer manuals provided with equipment.

Electronic Arts Foundation, Box 16, Freeport, NY 11520, telephone 516-378-4155. Contact Don Muro.

Conducts workshops for teachers and provides hands-on participation and learning opportunities for teachers.

PUBLICATIONS

Computers in Music, 647 Mission Street, San Francisco, CA 94105, telephone 415-541-5350.

Quarterly catalogue listing hardware and software that reviews new equipment and offers advice.

Electronic Musician, 6400 Hollis Street #12, Emeryville, CA 94608, telephone 510-653-3307.

Micro Music, Inc., 5353 Buford Highway, Atlanta, GA 30340, telephone 800-955-6434(MIDI); 404-454-9646.

Computer music retailer of software and hardware that offers an eight-week course on MIDI.

MIX Bookshelf Resource Guide, 6400 Hollis Street, #12, Emeryville, CA 94608, telephone 800-233-9604; 510-653-3307.

Catalog of professional resources for the audio and music recording industry.

Music and Computer Educator Magazine, 76 North Broadway, Hicksville, NY 11801, telephone 516-681-2922; fax 516-681-2926.

Forum for sharing of information by educators who use electronic equipment in the field.

The Technology Directory. Published by Association for Technology in Music Instruction (ATMI), an association for the development of computer systems. Contact Dr. Ann Blombach, Ohio State University, 110 Wiegel Hall, 1866 College Street, School of Music, Columbus, Ohio, 43210.

Software directory.

OTHER MENC PUBLICATIONS

Composition in the Classroom: A Tool for Teaching
Presents various techniques for teaching children skills to compose music under limited teacher guidance. The specific approaches examined are teacher-guided composition, which encourages children to work as a class to compose a song; small-group composition, which emphasizes working together in groups to create a composition using a specific element of music; and individual composition, in which children can create music on their own. Appropriate for elementary and junior high school levels. By Jackie Wiggins. 1990. 48 pages.

Teaching General Music: A Course of Study
Offers music teachers a model for developing a strong program of instruction for teaching courses in general music. Covers all levels from preschool to high school; outlines aspects of the curriculum including performing/reading, creating, listening/describing, and valuing; and offers objectives and procedures within each topic. Developed by the MENC Task Force on General Music Course of Study. 1991. 40 pages.

TIPS: Technology for Music Educators
Students can now learn to create music and communicate in musical ways by using synthesizers, videodiscs, and electronic keyboards. Presents ideas for using these new technologies as learning vehicles. Compiled by Charles G. Boody. 1990. 48 pages.

Choral Music for Children
An annotated list of works composed or arranged for the unchanged treble voice. Examines wide variety of musical styles; describes the music's characteristic qualities, form, style, and value for education; provides tips for teaching and presentation; and presents cross-references by composer, title, voicing, and level of difficulty. Includes listings for choral music both in English and foreign languages, indicating when foreign texts are supplemented by English versions. Edited by Doreen Rao. 1990. 176 pages.

For complete ordering information on these and other MENC resources, contact MENC Member Services:

By mail at 1806 Robert Fulton Drive, Reston, VA 20191
By phone at 1-800-828-0229 or 703-860-4000
By fax at 703-860-2652

Or visit the MENC Home Page on the Internet: http://www.menc.org
For fast service, credit card holders may call 1-800-828-0229,
Monday-Friday, 8:00a.m.-4:00p.m.

1047-10-1.5M-12/91